# NATIVE AMERICANS OF NORTH AMERICA

## PLATEAU REGION:
# YAKAMA PEOPLE

by
## Mary Null Boulé

Illustrated by
Daniel Liddell

Merryant Publishers, Inc.
Vashon, WA 98070
206-463-3879

A Series of Books

This series is dedicated to Virginia Harding, whose editing expertise and friendship brought this project to fruition.

**ISBN: 1-877599-52-2**

Copyright © 1997, Merryant Publishing

7615 S.W. 257th St., Vashon, WA 98070.

# FOREWORD

Native American people of the United States are often living their lives away from major cities and away from what we call the mainstream of life. It is, then, interesting to learn of the important part these remote tribal members play in our everyday lives.

More than 60% of our foods come from the ancient Native American's diet. Farming methods of today also can be traced back to how tribal women grew crops of corn and grain. Many of our present day ideas of democracy have been taken from tribal governments. Even some 1,500 Native American words are found in our English language today.

Fur traders bought furs from tribal hunters for small amounts of money, sold them to Europeans and Asians for a great deal of money, and became rich. Using their money to buy land and to build office buildings, some traders started business corporations which are now the base of our country's economy.

There has never been enough credit given to these early Americans who took such good care of our country when it was still in their care. The time has come to realize tribal contributions to our society today and to give Native Americans not only the credit, but the respect due them.

Mary Boulé

*A-frame cradle for*
*girls; tule matting.*
*Tubatulabal tribe.*

# NATIVE AMERICANS OF NORTH AMERICA
## INTRODUCTION

Creation legends told by today's tribal people speak of how, a very long time ago, their creator placed them in a territory where they became caretakers of that land and its animals. None of their ancient legends tells about the first Native Americans coming from another continent.

These tribal legends do not agree with the beliefs of anthropologists (scientific historians who study the habits and customs of humans). Clues found by anthropologists, and other scientists, lead them to believe that ancient tribespeople came to North America from Asia during the Ice Age period, between 20 and 35 thousand years ago.

Since none of us today lived thousands of years ago, our understanding of ancient people must come from studying clues; for example, tools and other artifacts left by people living then and from stories they have passed on from one generation to the next. It is important to respect the different beliefs and theories, to learn from and seek the truth in all of them.

Scientists' theories tell of people making their way across a narrow strip of land in the Bering Straits which, at one time, might have connected the Asian continent to land that is now the state of Alaska. It is thought that as ice from

*Caribou herds could well have been one kind of animal herd archeologists believe led human beings to the North American Continent*

4

Ice Age glaciers melted, it caused ocean waters to rise and cover the land bridge separating the two continents.

If such theories are correct, it is possible these people never knew they were crossing onto another continent, they were simply hunting for food. Because food was the most important need, these groups kept moving as they followed animal herds that were also on the move in search of food.

Scientists date the first people arriving on this continent to about 14,000 years ago. According to them, by the end of the Ice Age, over ten thousand years ago, many thousands of native peoples had settled in North America. According to the Native Americans' legends, they have been here, always.

Siberia

*Scientists' theories of how human beings might have migrated to this continent. Dotted arrow shows a recent scientific theory about how some ancient people from Europe may have come.*

# THE GROUPING OF NATIVE AMERICANS

Scientists say the earliest people coming from Asia probably traveled south through the center part of present-day Canada, dividing as they came near today's boundary between Canada and the United States. Some groups moved toward the Atlantic Coast, some continued south, while other groups migrated west toward the Pacific Coast. Most of them went to either the east or west coasts, possibly because of the wealth of seafood found in oceans.

Some tribal bands settled in the northwestern corner of this country, along the Pacific Coast. Probably the largest numbers claimed territory just south of the Northwest coastline, in a region known today as California. Both of these regions rewarded those who lived in them with much food, enough natural resources to clothe them and give them a good life.

Many other groups settled in the Great Lakes area of northeastern United States. The lakes, woods, and animals found there provided for everyday tribal needs. Those Native Americans who lived in the food-rich grassy plains in the center of our country also had plenty to eat. Eastern people grew fields of corn and squash and built large, permanent villages.

Those people who settled in the Plains region probably did so because of the hundreds of thousands of buffalo there. Plains groups depended upon the buffalo for food and clothing, before white people arrived, following the animals as they grazed.

Plateau tribes were fortunate their territory had large rivers (the Columbia and the Snake rivers) which furnished them with fish and some larger animals that could live in the extremes of climate found there.

*Redwood dugout canoe.*

# STUDYING ANCIENT PEOPLE

According to archeologists, as the early people moved in many directions to settle in the new continent, their ways of life and customs became different, one group from another. To help make their research simpler, historians who study human life usually divide those ancient people into groups. Some arrange their studies according to how certain groups found their food, giving them names like 'hunters,' 'seed gatherers,' 'diggers,' 'fishermen,' and 'farmers'—those who grew their own food.

Other historians divide Native Americans into study groups according to the language they spoke. Some of the mysteries of how tribes moved into North America have been solved by comparing the language spoken by a tribe in one area with that spoken in another place.

Although their accents might not be alike, basic words for objects or animals sometimes were found to be the same. This could mean that at one time two clans, having finally settled hundreds of miles apart, might once have lived close to each other. In such a case, this could show what path a tribe might have taken to reach its location.

One of these paths was along water. Tribespeople found traveling by water was easier than by land, at least until a few hundred years ago, when horses arrived on this continent with European explorers. Mostly, ancient villages were built on the banks of rivers, streams, and lakes, as well as near oceans.

Living near streams or lakes meant that villagers could visit neighboring settlements without having to walk long distances. Therefore, the same language usually was spoken in different villages found along one river. However dialects, or accents, of the main language would change from village to village. Those accents were like the differences we notice between a Southern accent and a New York accent.

Eventually, as groups of villagers moved farther away from each other, their language changed by adding names given to unknown objects they found in their new territory, or by inventing and naming different tools or clothing needed in the new land.

Many historians divide their study of ancient humans by geographic area, knowing that where settlements were found decided a tribe's way of life. Besides studying the language of a certain place, they like to learn what kind of village life people had, what materials they used to build their homes, the foods they ate, what types of tools they used. This kind of study is a more complete way to learn of human life long ago.

Therefore, we shall divide the North American continent into eight geographic areas and study ancient Native Americans according to where they lived. Below is a list of the eight regional names we will use:

1. Arctic and 1A. Subarctic

2. Northwest Coast

3. California

4. Southwest

5. Plateau and 5A. Basin

6. Plains

7. Eastern Woodlands

8. Southeast

## ARCTIC AND SUBARCTIC REGION

Hundreds of years after the first groups of settlers arrived on this continent, people we call Eskimos arrived near the North Pole in the Arctic region. The territory these newcomers claimed as their own was a narrow strip of land along the coast of the Arctic Ocean, from Alaska's Aleutian Islands east to Greenland. Even though their land was stretched out and Eskimos villages were far from each other, it is interesting to find that most of their customs, language, and clothing were the same.

Tribespeople in frozen Arctic land lived a very hard life because of severe winter cold and short summer seasons. During the few months of warm weather, they hunted caribou that lived in herds on land. Bows and arrows were used to kill land animals. Much of the caribou meat was preserved for winter meals by drying it into something like our modern-day 'jerky.'

Using bone needles, women sewed clothing from the skins of land animals. So great were the chances of Eskimos freezing to death, that during cold months they covered their entire bodies with warm clothing made of many different kinds of animal skins and fur. Eskimos always had to wear gloves, footwear, and hoods, even in summertime.

Although caribou meat was an important part of their diet, Eskimos depended on sea animals for their main food. Meat of whales, walruses, and seals contained great amounts of fat and oil, and fatty meat helped keep Eskimo bodies warm .

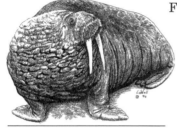

A walrus, one of the large sea mammals important to arctic and subarctic people for food, oil, and clothing.

Fishing for such large sea mammals was risky for tribal fishermen. They fished from kayaks, small one-person skin canoes, with the fishermen using only hand-thrown harpoons.

Most tools in this region were made of antler and tusk ivory, bone, or slate.

In ancient times, people in the coldest part of Eskimo territory built igloos, made of hand-cut chunks of ice, for winter homes. During the summer, villagers lived in skin tents. Farther inland, in the warmest areas, homes were built as much as six feet into the ground. The part of the house aboveground was usually made of stone, logs, and packed dirt.

The prefix 'sub' means below, or under something, so the word Subarctic means found below, or south, of the Arctic region. Subarctic tribes were found just south of Eskimo land, in what is today known as Canada. Although they had almost as much cold weather as did the Eskimos, their territory had great forests of spruce trees and thousands of freshwater lakes and rivers.

Tribes there depended on caribou and moose for their main food. Animals were herded into large fenced areas or caught in traps, then killed with bows and arrows or with spears. Native Americans in this region ate a lot of freshwater fish and, during the summer, women gathered berries, roots, and green plants for food. Because hunting was so difficult in winter's bitter cold, summer -caught meat and fish were preserved for winter meals.

Subarctic tribes used wood and bark from nearby forests to build homes and to make most tools and weapons. Those bands not close to forests made their tipi (sometimes spelled teepee) homes of pole framework, with caribou or moose hides forming the walls. Still other groups made dome-shaped (round) skin homes with pole frameworks.

Subarctic people dressed in animal skins from head to toe, just as the Eskimos did. They traveled on foot, wearing snowshoes throughout winter months. The usual way of traveling in the summer was by canoe.

*An animal skin kayak (canoe) used in the Arctic Ocean by Eskimos.*

## NORTHWEST COAST REGION

This region stretches along the Pacific Ocean coast from Alaska to as far south as northern California. Although coastal tribes in the far north had very cold weather during the winter, most Northwest tribes lived in a milder climate. Warm ocean currents caused rainy weather in the region but it was not often cold. Large forests of evergreen trees covered this land, giving tribes-people all the wood they needed. There are forests remaining today in this area which still look as they looked to ancient Northwest peoples.

Cedar bark, wood, and even evergreen tree boughs were used to make everything from fabric for clothing to huge homes (called long houses). Many related families lived in one house, which was decorated with tall totem poles in the more northern parts of the region. These totem poles were carved with symbols telling about the history of families living in the house.

Because it had at least an eight-month growing season, this land was rich with plants, fruits, and berries. Lakes and rivers were full of fish, especially the tasty salmon. Animals of all sizes lived in and around the forests, supplying Northwest tribes with nearly everything they needed to live a good life.

*Log home of the northern coastal Tlingit people.*

*Northwest coast woman wearing a shawl made of cedar bark.*

## CALIFORNIA REGION

California is an area of many different climates. The taller, eastern Sierra mountains form today's California-Nevada border. A coastal range of lower mountains runs along the ocean side of this region. Winters in the highest mountains are very cold, with snow covering the land all winter. Between the mountain ranges lies the long San Joaquin Valley. It is very hot in the summer but mostly pleasant and warm in the valley for the rest of the year.

The southern area of the California region, except along the coast and in the higher mountains, was desert, with sparse cactus plants and trees and very little water. Climate in the lowlands was warm for most of the year, and very hot in the summer.

Valley homes were usually built into the ground a few feet to keep them cooler in the summer and warmer in the winter. Dwellings were built over a framework of bendable branches and covered with woven mats made of tule grass or with cross-sticks covered with dirt. In the mountains, homes were dug deeper into the ground to protect tribal people from the much colder climate, and dirt was placed on top of the branch roofs.

California tribes had good weather in some part of their territory all year long. Many tribes moved to the mountains in summertime and to lower land in the winter, but others only left their permanent villages a few times a year, when they gathered acorns or visited lakes or the ocean to fish.

California people ate everything from plants, roots, and berries, to land animals and sea food. Their basic food, however, was acorn nuts from the five or six different kinds of oak trees growing throughout their land.

*Tule mat home of central California.*

12

*One of the six different varieties of oak trees growing in what is California, today.*

Since all but the inland-southern California Native Americans had enough food nearby all year long, they did not have to spend all day, every day, hunting for something to eat. For instance, California tribal women in most areas found time to make beautiful baskets, while men along the coast had time to build amazing seagoing, wood-plank boats that were strong enough to go great distances away from the ocean shore. The planks in these boats were actually sewn together with sinew, stretchy animal tendons.

One tribe used its plank boats to make the 20-mile trip through the Pacific Ocean to Santa Catalina Island. There they mined a soft soapstone rock called steatite, which could be carved into useful items like bowls, pots, and cooking griddles.

It is no wonder the California region had some of the largest numbers of Native Americans found on the whole continent; life there was good.

## PLATEAU AND BASIN REGIONS

Life was not at all easy in the Basin region, one of the driest parts of our country. Basin tribes, especially, suffered. Their territory was found where Utah and Nevada are today. Winters were fiercely cold and summers were very hot. The land was covered with rocks and sand but few plants and fewer trees, because it almost never rained.

In the frigid winters, Basin people lived in homes dug into the ground a few feet. A framework of small willow-tree branches formed the roofs and walls, which were then covered with bark, cattails, or grass. These houses looked like upside-down ice cream cones. During the summer, however, only brush shelters were needed for homes, mainly to keep tribal members out of the sun.

*Example of homes built by native peoples of the Basin region.*

Few tribes lived in this region, since it took a great deal of land to find enough plants to feed even one group of people. As a result, tribelets were scattered far from each other, and every day, all day, was spent hunting for food. Basin people either faced risky trips into enemy Plains tribes' territories, to hunt for their buffalo meat, or had to learn to live on less animal meat.

Rather than be killed by Plains warriors for trespassing, in order to kill buffalo, many Basin groups chose to eat roots, and whatever else they could find that grew in their hostile desert region. Pine nuts and small animals, such as rodents (rabbits, prairie dogs, rats, field mice) made up most of their diet. Yet insects, snakes, fish from the region's few lakes, and birds were also important foods. Basin tribes often had to move to new places when food in one area ran out.

Clothing was not needed by Basin region men and children during the hot summers, but women wore apron-like skirts of animal skin or strips of bark all year long. In the bitter-cold winter, tribespeople wore short capes of woven rabbit skins that came down to their waists. Sometimes men wore pieces of animal skin, sewn together and tied at the waist, to form a skirt. When there were no animal skins for clothing, feathered duckskins were used.

North of the Basin area is the Plateau region, where Eastern Washington, Eastern Oregon, Idaho, and Montana are today.

14

Tribes there also worked hard, at times, to find enough food to eat, since the climate was arid (dry) and the winters bitterly cold. Mostly their diet was made up of large-animal meat, roots of desert plants, wild berries, and fish from lakes and rivers.

Some low mountain ranges in the area grew scrub pine trees, furnishing wood the villagers could use for house framework. The huge Columbia and Snake Rivers were the most important natural resources in the region, providing fish for food and transportation for trading along the riverbanks.

Homes for the earliest of these native peoples were called pithouses. Often round, the base of the houses were dug into the ground a few feet, with a dirt-covered log framework on top. Later, after the tribes had horses, most plateau people made very large winter lodges with pole framework and woven mat walls so they easily could be hauled from place to place. Many families lived in each lodge, which was shaped like a long tent.

*Unique style of home built by the Yakama villagers of the Plateau region.*

**SOUTHWEST REGION**

The Southwest region tribes were located in what is today Arizona, New Mexico, and Texas. Little water could be found there, and few plants besides cactus could stay alive in that dry country; a true desert climate.

In spite of their desert territory, Native American people of this region made good use of what was found around them. A few Southwest tribes roamed from place to place looking for food and living in simple shelters of piled brush, but most tribes lived all year in clusters or in actual cities. City homes were built several stories high, like apartments, with thick, baked clay (called adobe)

15

*A village of adobe (hard baked clay) homes built in the Southwest region.*

walls to keep out the fierce summer sun. These kinds of homes were called *pueblos.*

Pueblo people could stay in one place all year because they farmed their own food. Fields of maize (corn) were grown in the rich, dry, sandy soil, as well as beans, sunflowers, and squash. The villagers irrigated their fields with underground water. Usually, the only kind of animal meat eaten was rabbit.

Since the men of these tribes farmed their own food, they did not have to spend their days hunting or fishing. Therefore, they had time to weave wild cotton into fabric, while women spent their free time making baskets and fine, beautiful pottery.

## PLAINS REGION

What we call the western plains of our country are the modern states of Kansas, Nebraska, and North and South Dakota. The western half of the Plains region was flat, treeless prairie land, covered with short grass. Buffalo liked the grass-covered land of this region, and Plains tribespeople liked the buffalo. Never ones to waste food, the Native Americans used almost every part of a buffalo. It provided them with food, clothing, tools, weapons, and hides for tipi walls.

Buffalo were so important to many Plains tribes that many groups did not build villages but lived in camps, following buffalo herds as the animals roamed the land. Some tribes, however, did build dirt lodges rather than move from place to place.

When white settlers arrived, they deliberately killed most of the buffalo. These animals were not killed for food or clothing for

16

the settlers, however; the settlers killed the Native Americans' main source of food to force them to leave. It greatly changed the way of life for those tribespeople who had depended on the buffalo.

Tall grass grew in many wooded areas found on the region's eastern side, which today includes the states of Iowa, Ohio, and Missouri. At one time, about 3,000 years ago, the eastern side of the Plains region was settled by people called 'mound- builders.' These bands of Native Americans built huge permanent villages along the Mississippi River and farmed their land for food.

Because they did not have to hunt for food, mound- builders found time to make huge hills of dirt, some of which were used as burial places for important tribal members. Beautiful objects like carved birds and animals have been found inside the burial mounds.

Other mounds were used as bases for religious temples, much like those built in Mexico and South America by the Mayans and the Aztecs. For this reason, many anthropologists believe the mound-builders probably migrated from Central America, where older mounds, built much like those in the Plains region, have been discovered. Some of the Plains base mounds, still standing in present day Ohio and Missouri, are over 1,000 feet long, 700 feet wide, and 100 feet high.

*Plains tipi, made of animal skins, could be easily moved from place to place.*

*Elm bark long house of the Northeast Woodland Region.*

## NORTHEAST WOODLAND REGION

This region extends from the modern state of Wisconsin east to the Atlantic Coast. Forests of birch, pine, and elm trees grow here. Native Americans farmed, hunted for deer, and fished in the hundreds of lakes and rivers found in this woodlands area. Food was plentiful most of the year.

Northernmost Woodlands tribes lived in large elm-bark long houses during the summer and mat-covered, dome-shaped lodges in the winter. Others, in the region's southern areas, lived in wigwam homes built of pole-and-branch frames bound together with cedar bark, and having walls of birch bark or grass mats.

Many groups of this region depended more on the crops they grew for food than on meat of animals they found living in nearby forests. Crops of squash, corn, and beans furnished the people with food all year long. So important were these three foods, villagers called them 'the three sisters' and devoted special religious ceremonies of thanks to them during the year.

In the most northern parts of this region, however, farming was much more difficult because of long, bitter-cold winters and short growing seasons. There tribespeople depended more on hunting and fishing for their food. In places near the Atlantic Ocean, both saltwater and freshwater fishing provided villagers with food.

## SOUTHEAST REGION

The Southeast region includes what is present-day Florida, Georgia, North and South Carolina, Mississippi, Louisiana, and Arkansas. There may have been as many as fifty clans of people living in this area, many of them probably mound-builders who had moved south from the center of the continent.

Since these Native Americans were farmers, their villages were permanent. Everyone in the tribe helped with farm work, even the children, who scared away crows from the planted seeds. Climate in the most southeastern part of this region (Florida) was warm most of the year, so homes were not much more than shelters with grass-mat roofs. Winter homes, placed beside summer shelters, had mat walls and contained kitchens.

Men and children seldom wore clothing, but for ceremonies the men dressed in colorful robes of woven bird feathers. Women wore deerskin skirts all year; in winter they added a short dress on top of the skirt. Moccasins were worn only for ceremonies or for travel.

European explorers arrived in the Southeast Region so long ago that original village life of these Native Americans has been long forgotten. Much of what we learn about these tribespeople comes from artifacts archeologists (those who study the belongings of ancient people) find buried in dirt at old village sites and from tribal stories handed down from generation to generation.

*Seminole village of the Southeast Region.*

19

## WHAT THEY LOOKED LIKE

When European explorers began landing on these shores almost four hundred years ago, they thought all Native American people were of the same race, but many experts today do not agree. Certainly not all Native Americans looked alike.

For instance, most members of the Plains tribes were quite tall with large craggy heads and long thin noses. They looked like the heads we see on Indianhead nickels. And yet, one coastal California tribe had rounder, flatter noses, and the men were not much taller than five feet. Southwest tribes were shorter than Plains tribespeople. Some tribes had darker skin, others had almost white skin.

Most Native Americans of the early times had dark brown eyes, high cheekbones, very straight black hair, and were heavily tanned from living outside most of the time. It is interesting to note that very few Native American men had facial hair. Men of only a few tribes had enough facial hair to grow beards or mustaches, and yet there are few bald Indian men, to this day.

## TOOLS, UTENSILS, AND WEAPONS

To supply their needs, Native Americans always used objects of nature found around them. Plants furnished food, fiber from its stalks for rope, healing herbal teas from plant leaves for medicines, and brushes, as well as shampoo, from

*Large, twined seed-gatherer's burden basket made by the fine basket weavers of the California Pomo tribe.*

20

some plant roots. Grasses growing around villages were made into mats for dwelling walls and used for weaving baskets.

Usually the women made baskets for their families, but men of some tribes were known to be excellent basketmakers. Baskets were needed for cooking, storage, and for gathering food. Some California tribal weavers wove their large storage baskets so tightly, they were used as boats, carrying belongings, even children across rivers and lakes.

Animal bones were made into eating utensils (men of one clan used moose elbows as spoons); music instruments and whistles; bone splinters for sewing needles; pointed pieces as tips for arrows; and even the front teeth of beavers (sometimes the whole upper jaw) were used to scrape wood. The antlers of larger animals, such as antelope and elk, became wedges for splitting logs into planks for the exterior walls of homes.

By the time European explorers arrived on this continent, Native American hunters were using bows and arrows. Before bows and arrows, hunters only had an atlatl, (at lat' ul) to launch their spears, when they hunted for larger animals.

*One of the finest bows made by Native Americans, this Achumawi bow has been copied by championship archers today.*

Tribal hunters found bows and arrows to be far better weapons than atlatls because arrows could travel farther and faster than a hand-thrown spear. Not only were animals more likely to be killed by the speed of an arrow, but a hunter's life was safer the farther away from his target he could stay. The far-flying arrow let him remain a safer distance from animals he stalked.

It was not a simple job to make bows that would not break and arrows that flew straight to a target. When constructing a bow,

hunters looked for strong, bendable wood that was not brittle or easily broken. Often animals' stretchy tendons (called sinew) were wrapped around a bow to keep it from breaking when bent.

Because of this need for a supple bow, most hunters did not string their bows until the last moment, as they ran toward an animal they needed to kill. Their bows lasted much longer that way.

Good hunters spent months making their bows and arrows. They needed lightweight hardwood that did not bend easily to form arrow shafts. Even after weapons were finished, it was necessary to spend several days before a hunt re-straightening arrow shafts. Using heat, water, and a grooved stone, a hunter made sure his arrows would fly in a true direction.

Some tribal women made mortars and pestles from wood for crushing soft herbs they made into medicinal teas to cure sick people. Many warriors wore wooden-pole vests as armor when fighting wars. Some clever Native Americans used sharkskin as sandpaper when smoothing wood objects.

Stone was another important natural resources to Native Americans. Stone mortars and pestles were constantly used by village women to grind grains into flour. Some arrow tips were fashioned from stone.

*Stone mortar and pestle for crushing grains into flour.*

Volcanic glass made into the best arrowheads since it was strong and had very sharp edges when shaped with a stone flaking tool. Volcanic glass also was used as knife blades by both men and women.

# VILLAGE LIFE

Each group of Native Americans had its own customs, laws, and form of government. Many still follow the ancient laws of their ancestors. It was the custom of Eastern North American tribes, for example, to consider a woman's family as the most important. Families were placed on a family tree according to the woman's name and her relatives. Western tribes often gave such importance to a man's family name and his relatives.

Where one tribe might have many chiefs, another would have no chief. Some tribes had so many villages of people, a council was formed made up of chiefs from each village, to lead the entire tribal nation. Other groups were not well organized but allowed each village of relatives to be led by its own chief.

Religious beliefs were seldom the same among Native Americans, but almost all groups worshipped one guardian spirit they believed created them and looked out for their well being. This guardian was thought to be supernatural and to have power which could be found in sacred places. Some groups felt the creator would punish them if they did not follow tribal law.

Most village religions were based on the belief that wild animals found around them also had supernatural powers, which might explain why animal names were used for family names. Certain birds or animals had special spiritual meaning to most groups.

Among supernatural creatures, most tribes believed eagles had the greatest power. Therefore, families taking the name of Eagle usually were those serving as leaders in village government. Chiefs were usually members of the Eagle family, for example.

Coyote was important in many bands, or tribes, also. Coyote was both a good and bad spirit, making him more like humans, so he was usually well-liked by tribal members. Bears were greatly feared by most Native Americans, and some tribes would not even eat bear meat. There were other tribes, however, with secret bear societies that would use the villagers' fear of them as a power to control people.

Large, important religious ceremonies were held during the year to honor god-spirits. Villagers, wearing bright, beautiful costumes, performed rituals at such ceremonies. Visitors from neighboring tribes attended them. Sometimes the ceremony included traders who brought items to trade for things they wanted from the host tribe. Often there were great athletic competitions and games played at these festivities.

*Headdress for the Big Head ceremonies, Lake and Coast Miwok tribes.*

Traders were the links between different tribes. They moved from territory to territory, bringing items of value from their own tribe to use in trade for items their home tribe needed or wanted.

Traders also shared any good ideas and news they learned in distant villages.

# FINDING A MODERN NAME

It is known that early European settlers arriving in this country called those original (first) tribespeople either 'Indians' or 'Red Men.' Actually, they were neither red-skinned, nor were they Indians. Many believe it was Christopher Columbus who first called Native Americans 'Indians.' In 1492, when he landed on an island near modern-day Florida, Columbus thought he had reached the country of India, so he called the islanders he found living there 'Indians.'

No one knows for sure how the phrase 'Red Men' came to be. However, many historians think European explorers were responsible for the incorrect name. To honor European visitors, friendly tribespeople greeted them dressed in colorful ceremonial clothing and wearing bright body paints. Since dyes used for body paints were often red, explorers again got the wrong idea, giving Native Americans the added incorrect name of 'Red Men.'

When modern descendants (relatives) of those first Americans recently decided to pick their own name, many chose to be called *Native* Americans. The word *native* means to be born, grow, and live in one place. The word *native* also means to live **naturally** in a place without changing it. That is, to use only what nature has provided to satisfy the needs for food, clothing, and shelter. Nothing more.

For the 14,000 years that Native Americans were the only ones taking care of this land, they treated it well. Most of them killed only as many animals as were needed for food and clothing. In their care, the land remained healthy.

In the past four hundred years, as white people began to manufacture products that would make their lives easier, our environment began to suffer. Factories and their products now pollute our water, air, and land. Metal, plastic, and rubber, among other waste products, have added great piles of garbage to Planet Earth that do not break down and disappear into the soil, as natural-product waste does.

*A California Chumash shaman dressed in ceremonial clothing, with his body painted in red designs.*

Changing nature itself to make our lives easier has caused many problems, some—but not all—of them too large for us to correct. Even more serious, poisoning the area around us has harmed animals and fish, causing us to lose entire species of planet life. Unlike tribal people, we have not taken good care of the natural world.

Perhaps now it is easier to understand why there are North American Indians who have chosen to call themselves *Native* Americans. The good care they gave to our North American continent, before the explorers arrived, has truly earned them a right to add the word *native* to their name.

# CONCLUSION

Although much original tribal life has been lost since the arrival of the first explorers, many reminders of the ancient Native Americans are built into our modern life. Names of cities, towns, and streets often carry either the name of a famous tribal leader or are tribal words in themselves.

The city of Seattle, for example, was named for one of the beloved Salish tribal leaders, Chief Sealth. California's Hoopa Valley was named for the Hupa Tribe, who once owned the entire area. Lake Nokomis in Minnesota has a Native American name. Even the names of the states of Texas and (North and South) Dakota are Native American words; the words mean 'friend' in two different tribal languages.

Modern doctors prescribe as medicine some of the tribal herbs village shamans (doctors) once brewed to heal patients. European settlers learned from the Native Americans how to plant corn, squash, and beans for food. The settlers also learned how to change (rotate) crops each year so that soil in their fields would stay rich in minerals, and crops would remain large.

Not only did the Native Americans teach the white settlers how to grow corn, but they also shared their cooking recipes. To this day we still enjoy one of the best of those recipes: Popcorn!

Many Native Americans acted as guides when white people first began to explore and settle the western United States. One Native American woman, Sacajawea, has become famous in our history books for guiding white explorers, William Clark and Meriwether Lewis, safely across the northern part of the United States to the Pacific Ocean in 1804.

It would have been much better if settlers had realized that North American Indians already had claimed as their territory, the land where American pioneers chose to settle. Unlike white people, who marked their land with fences, Native Americans marked their territory by such natural landmarks as mountains or rivers or huge rocks, never with fences. Settlers, not seeing Indian fences, simply claimed tribal land as their own.

Even more serious, when Native American leaders asked for the return of sacred tribal cemetery grounds, and valuable grass-lands needed by native women for plant food and basketmaking materials, white pioneers, with legal papers from the federal government telling them the land was theirs, chose not to listen to tribal leaders' requests. It is no wonder many tribes fought fiercely for their lost territory.

Organized native nations today work hard to reclaim some of the territory they lost to settlers. Reclaiming their land is not the only project important to them. Many tribes are busy relearning and teaching the language of their people to their youngsters.

Tribal centers are found throughout the United States today, many of them quite large. Some of these centers have gathered together their own artifacts and built valuable museums to hold their findings. It is important to these leaders to present their beliefs from the tribal point of view. Native American centers show the pride these people have in their heritage by sharing their native life as it was before white people arrived, changing their land forever.

# THE YAKAMA NATION

## INTRODUCTION

North America's Plateau Region is bordered by the Rocky Mountains in the east and the Cascade Mountains in the west. Northern boundaries are marked by the Fraser River in what is today British Columbia. The Plateau southern boundaries are found mid-way through the states of Oregon and Idaho.

Scientists call this Plateau area 'semi-arid,' meaning the sandy ground offers sage brush, juniper shrubs, bunch grass, and some willow and cottonwood trees near streams. The land is too dry and hot in the summer to allow large forests to grow here but some scrub pines grow in clusters.

Since there were no large trees growing in this region, the sage brush became of great importance to tribal people. Sagebrush bark could be twisted into boxes or containers to hold belongings. If ever it was needed, ancient travelers knew they could bind together several sage bushes to make wind shelters from the often fierce winds.

The sagebrush plant also was used for medicines, to flavor drinks, and to form fabric for clothes. Tribal women pounded sage so it could be shredded and woven into a cloth for making pants, shirts, skirts, shoes, and sandals.

Today sagebrush, small animals, and rattlesnakes still live there in steep canyons and along river banks in the Plateau Region. Larger animals used to live on the eastern slopes of the mountains, where sparse forests of pine trees grew. However, fewer large animals are found there these days because much of the desertlike land has become irrigated farmland.

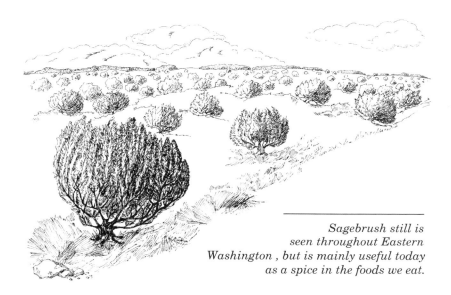

*Sagebrush still is seen throughout Eastern Washington , but is mainly useful today as a spice in the foods we eat.*

Plateau climate never has been an easy one in which to live. There are four definite seasons in the region but summer temperatures climb to well over 100°F and remain that high for weeks at a time. During the long dark winters, temperatures fall well below zero°F, and deep layers of snow usually cover the ground for months at a time.

The land was rich with natural resources, but because of such extremes in weather and little rain, Plateau Native Americans did not find their region good for farming. During most of the year, they had to move from one food-gathering camp to another.

Neither animals nor humans can live without water and, fortunately, this region has two huge river systems: the Fraser and the Columbia Rivers and all the many streams and rivers which flow into them. The two river systems were nature's life-giving gifts to native people living in this semi-arid land.

Waterways provided ancient Plateau people with fish for food, water to drink, and a 'highway' upon which to travel great distances. River travel was especially important to tribespeople before European horses arrived with explorers in the 1700s. Horses meant people no longer had to walk from place to place on land.

One band of people depending on the mighty Columbia River system was the Yakima, or Yakama (Yak' uh maw) tribe. The name Yakama has been spelled many ways through the years, but in recent times modern tribal members have chosen to spell the name of their nation Yakama, with an "a" instead of an "i."

The Yakamas did not name themselves. As with most Native American tribes, they simply called themselves 'the people.' Neighboring villagers who spoke the Salish language used words to name the Yakamas that sounded like *Yahahkimas* or *Eyakimas*. Usually such names were descriptions of where a group lived.

Yakama people today think the word Yakama sounds a great deal like *'eyakina,'* a word meaning 'more than one bear.' There is a tribal legend, passed down through the years, telling a story of three small bears playing on the banks of the Columbia River. Since that could be a description of one part of Yakima territory, the bear theory seems to make sense.

The Yakamas lived in a part of the plateau area we now call Eastern Washington. Historians have found tools and other belongings that show these people have been living on some part of their land for at least 12,000 years.

For centuries a Yakama legend of how the people came to be on this earth has been told to young tribal members by village elders. The story tells of how Creator first made the earth and then put living things upon it. After placing living things on Earth, the Creator then created people to live in certain places.

The Yakamas' Creator legend explains how all the land where they and their ancestors have lived was created just for them. It also makes clear that people must never think of themselves as more important than the plants or wild animals living around them.

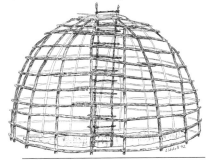

*Frame for the house on page 31.*

# VILLAGES

Because tribal people moved to food-gathering places during most of the year, villages with permanent homes were used only during winter. The rest of the year villagers lived in brush shelters at food camps.

Yakama permanent villages were usually found in clusters along river valleys. Valley walls protected the villagers from winter's bitterly cold winds, and the largest rivers gave them water all year long. Besides the settlement itself, hunting and gathering territory was a part of any village. Size of a territory was decided by how many animals and plants were needed to feed those living in the village. Most Yakamas were quite generous, sharing their hunting and gathering lands with needy neighbors.

Clues found by anthropologists show that the ancient Yakama tribal nation numbered some 7,000 people, who lived in 60 to 70 permanent villages. Many of these villages were found where the Yakima River meets the Columbia River. Umatilla and Walla Walla tribes also had permanent villages there.

Other studies show that, at one time, nearly 2,400 people living in 120 lodges (homes), divided into several permanent settlements just north of where the Snake River flows into the Columbia.

An average village population ranged from 50 to 200 people, although some villages were much larger. The largest village was thought

*Ancient pit-house with door opening in the top. By digging several feet into the ground before putting up the framework of a house, the ground walls kept a home warmer in the winter and cooler in the summer.*

to have had a population of close 2,000 people and was found near today's town of Union Gap (near the present-day city of Yakima.)

Each permanent village was made up of homes (or lodges), sweat lodges, and usually small huts known as birthing huts, where young women gave birth to their babies. Most villages, especially the smaller ones, were made up of people related to each other.

The earliest homes were known as pit houses because, when building the house, first a round, or circular pit, 12 to 18 feet across, was dug into the ground to a depth of three or four feet. A framework of lightweight wooden poles was placed over the top of the pit. The frame was then covered with reed mats made of tule cane, followed by a layer of grass, and finally with up to three feet of dirt over the grass.

Each pit house had an opening in the rounded top which was used both as a smoke hole and as an entrance to the house. Steps cut into a pole made a ladder for entering or leaving the house.

Later, in the early 1700s, the style of Yakama homes changed to an **A**-shape building with several layers of bound tule, reed, or cattail mats used for walls. The reason probably was that horses had become a part of tribal life; Plateau people found that horses could pull a small, cone-shaped version of the new-style mat house to food-gathering camps more easily than the older-style house.

Often the traveling house had animal-skin walls instead of mats, so it weighed less. A house framework had to be moved from camp to camp. The usual way to do this was to haul it on a *travois*— a sled-like object made of two poles, to which a mat had been tied. House walls and poles were placed on the mat and dragged across the ground by an animal.

Before horses, dogs were used to pull the loads. The arrival of horses made traveling to a new camp much simpler and faster, since horses could carry heavier loads than dogs.

Large permanent mat lodges were found in winter villages. They ranged from 40 to 60 feet long and were from 12 to 15 feet wide

*This type of long mat-walled home was like no other found in what is present-day United States.*

at floor level. Mat sidewalls sloped to a point at the top and were often ten feet above the ground at the highest point. Small poles were attached over the mats, on the outside, to keep them in place.

Smoke holes were left in the very top of a lodge. A lodge door was put in one of the front or back **A**-shaped end walls, which were rounded outward.

Few pieces of furniture were found inside a Yakama lodge. There were no seating benches or storage shelves. An aisle went down the center of the lodge where the family cooking fires were placed. A fire was used by two families, one on each side of it. Every family had its own sleeping area next to the fire. Belongings of a family were kept in its sleeping area.

Another kind of building found in villages was the sweathouse. It was always built close to a stream. Usually the building was quite small and dome-shaped. Framework was most often made of young willow branches bent over a shallow, hollowed-out spot on the ground. When its walls were covered with mats and dirt it formed the shape of half an orange. Fir and cedar boughs covered the floor around the hollowed-out place.

*Frame for a sweathouse which were kept small so heat and steam could build up more rapidly.*

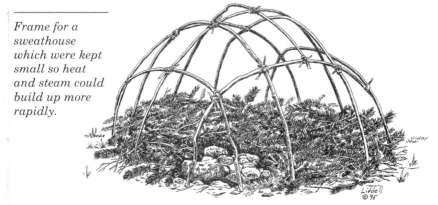

Outside the sweat lodge, large stones were placed in a hollow so they could be heated with fire when needed. After the stones were hot they were raked into the hollow of a sweathouse floor. The sweathouse entrance was then sealed shut, and those inside began to throw drops of water onto the stones to form clouds of steam. As you can see, a sweat house was much like our modern-day sauna.

Songs were sometimes chanted by the bathers while they bathed. When steambathers could stand the heat no longer they would dash out of the sweatlodge and leap into the icy, running water to cool down. Villagers did this many times in a row before they felt both spiritually and physically clean and purified. Hunters always purified themselves this way before going on hunting trips.

Steam bathers felt that steam not only conditioned their bodies but cured sickness. When Yakamas were first mentioned in white peoples' journals, they were described as 'cleanly.'

# VILLAGE LIFE

Like any modern dwellers of a town or city today, villagers had their own special jobs. Young men and women often worked together. Men caught and trained horses, women packed the horses for travel. Women made the tule mats for longhouse walls, while men built a pole framework and attached the mats to it. Women also made the reed mats used for bedding, rugs, containers for storing food, and to line the inside walls of a home.

Men did the hunting, fishing, and building, while it was the job of the women to gather plants, roots, and berries for meals, preserve food for winter, make clothing, tan animal skins, and weave baskets. When there was a village festival, men prepared the meat for cooking. Women villagers carried firewood and water needed to feed the many guests attending a festival.

Rather than seeing their band as a small part of one huge tribe, tribal members tended to think of their village as an independent group of people, able to take care of themselves.

It was important to villagers that they solve their own problems. Only very small villages with no leaders went to larger neighboring villages for advice or help, when it was needed.

Usually the job of chief was inherited from father to his finest son. However, when a village chief had to be chosen, villagers looked among themselves for a leader who was honest, generous, and had good speaking ability and good judgement. They especially looked for someone who had an even temper, so he could settle disputes and keep peace within his settlement.

A chief made the important decisions for his village. It was his duty to decide when to move to another food-gathering camp, or when to have a celebration and invite other villages. Although the chief or headman was usually a man, certain older women were highly respected and helped make village decisions, as well.

Village leaders often had specials skills: for instance the best hunters, warriors, fishermen, athletes, basketweavers, root-diggers, and religious doctors (shamans) helped share the responsibility of running a village.

Many of these well-respected villagers were members of a village council. They were chosen by a chief to help him solve a community's problems. Sometimes trouble arose between villages. Often problems had to do with trespassers, those people who came onto Yakama land without permission. If there was trouble between two villages, leaders from each village met to solve the problem.

A chief also had an assistant who went through the village each evening shouting his chief's wise words and spreading any news of the day to villagers. Another important chief's helper was a man called the 'whipper,' whose job was to make village children behave, especially during religious ceremonies. At any time, however, parents might threaten to give their children's names to the 'whipper' if they felt their children were misbehaving.

Small villages usually had from five to fifteen lodges. Several sets of grandparents, parents and their children, all related, lived together in a lodge. Many tribes throughout North America honored only one side of a child's family. In the eastern part of the continent, many groups took the name of the mother's family. In California the father's family was honored. Yakama people honored both sides of a family as blood relatives, just as we do in America today.

After a young man and woman decided to marry, the families on both sides arranged all the details. Before a child was born, the young couple lived with either family, usually the woman's. Shortly after the first child was born, an event called the 'wedding trade' took place. The 'wedding trade' was rather like a marriage ceremony since it formally announced the marriage to others of the village.

At that time the bride's family invited the groom's family to a feast. The hosts would give the groom's family fine gifts. Women received baskets, decorated corn husk bags full of food like dried roots, and jewelry wrapped in a tule mat. Later the groom's family would put on a feast for the young woman's family; men's gifts, such as blankets and tanned animal skins, were wrapped in rawhide and presented to her family.

The new baby was born in a birthing hut. Soon after the child was born, it was placed in a wooden and buckskin cradleboard decorated with trinkets and colored stones. A hoop made of wild rosebush branches, thought to protect the child from harm, was

*Yakama cradleboard made of wood and covered with buckskin.*

often attached to the cradleboard over the baby's head. Before the age of three, children spent much of their time in cradleboards. As a baby grew, larger cradleboards were made for it.

The training of children was left to their grandparents, who were not as busy gathering food as the young adults were. Older people set a good example of proper behavior; they also taught Yakama youngsters to respect all village laws, to take care of themselves without help, and especially to respect the rights of others.

Children learned such wisdom as: *remember your grandparents' teachings; share your home; help one another;* and *the more you give, the more you receive.* These rules were part of the prayers children were taught by their village elders long ago. They still are excellent rules to live by today.

Grandparents were the storytellers of a village. Sitting around a fire in a longhouse during long winter evenings, old villagers retold tribal stories which had been told for hundreds of years. Legends were fun for children to listen to and a useful way to teach young tribal children the difference between right and wrong.

Legends also helped to explain village laws and to make youngsters understand the importance of bravery, goodness, and inner strength. Stories of what happened to people who behaved badly, or who were selfish or bragged about themselves, were a good way to teach tribal children what parents believed was proper behavior.

Animals usually were the main characters in these village legends. One favorite story character was Coyote. He was a trickster who could be very helpful to humans at times but, like humans, could also be very bad and be punished for his mistakes. Many legends were told to explain how things happened to be on our earth. One story tells of a mythical beaver who dug a channel so the Columbia River could make its way to the Pacific Ocean.

Figures from ancient legends have been found in petroglyphs (carved or painted pictures) on huge rocks along the banks of the Columbia River. The petroglyphs were done in rich colors of red, yellow, white, and blue and some have been there for

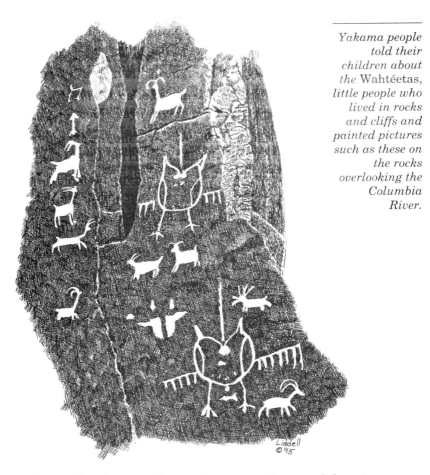

*Yakama people told their children about the* Wahtéetas, *little people who lived in rocks and cliffs and painted pictures such as these on the rocks overlooking the Columbia River.*

thousands of years. These picture carvings and drawings were believed to be done by 'little people' who lived in the rocks and cliffs. Artists were supposed to be seen only by children, and they could cause great danger to any adult who happened to see one.

The drawings and carvings show buffalo, deer, and other wild animals, as well as some of the spirits from tribal legends. Many of those spiritual characters are still included in modern Yakama legends. Although the meaning of some of the drawings has been lost over the past 200 years, Yakama tribal members know about certain important spirits, like Tsagiglalal (meaning She Who Watches).

'She Who Watches ' was drawn on a rock with reddish ochre-colored paint 200 to 250 years ago. In those days only religious people, such as shamans, were allowed to come near her picture because she was thought to be the messenger of death. Drawn in the shape of an owl, 'She Who Watches' was given huge eyes, straight, stick-up ears, a long nose, and a mouth with teeth gritted. Today her color has become faded from the environment but she can still be seen, looking toward the Columbia River.

While it was the grandparents' job to train the village young people, it was the parents' job to teach their children how to do many adult jobs. They did this by allowing the small ones to watch them at work. Boys learned about hunting, fishing, and such jobs as breaking wild horses. When a boy killed his first deer, a feast was held to celebrate his success.

Girls were taught how to gather certain roots, berries, and fruits. A special feast was given for a girl when she picked an extra-large basket of berries or dug many roots. Older girls also took care of the smaller children.

The learning of longer, harder jobs, like making bows and arrows or weaving baskets, was left to the grandparents, since they had more time for teaching difficult lessons. Such important jobs as collecting and cooking foods for their familes kept young adult villagers busy all day, everyday.

A boy became a man, in the eyes of his village, when he was able to do a man's work. Girls were considered adults when they became teenagers. At that time, a girl would begin a hempstring ball with knots or shell beads tied in it to remind her of certain special days in her life. The

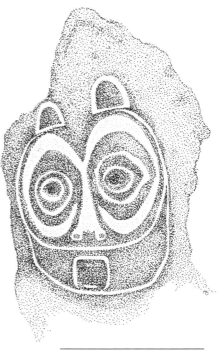

*She Who Watches.*

39

older a woman became, the larger the ball grew. Through her lifetime, the ball would be like written journals kept by many women today. The hempstring ball was then buried with her when she died.

When a villager died, relatives of the family gathered to help those loved ones closest to the dead person. Many relatives came great distances to attend a funeral. Just as today, visitors brought food and prepared meals.

Funeral rituals lasted five days and nights. Mourners sang songs to a drum beat as they stood around the body. It was hoped the songs would help a dead person's spirit safely reach its final resting place.

Dead bodies were then wrapped in skins tied with cords made of bark or grass, laid east to west in the earth, and the burial site was then marked with small wooden picket fences. Close relatives cut their hair short to show their sorrow.

After a body was buried, the dead person's house was burned in a special rite. It was thought that getting rid of the house would take away reminders of the dead relative, and make life easier for the still-living loved ones.

If the dead villager had been married, gifts were exchanged between both families of husband and wife. At the end of one year, the families once again shared gifts, marking an end to their mourning period. Once the mourning period was over, mourners could again begin attending village ceremonies and other events.

## CELEBRATIONS AND FEASTS

Not all ceremonies were sad like funerals. Yakama villagers were very social and organized many big get-togethers with other Northwest tribes. For instances, happy celebrations were

*A digging stick used by Yakama village women to uncover camas bulbs.*

held for first foods of a season and root-digging events probably were the biggest festivals to take place each year.

Celebrations like these were always shared with other villages and tribes. One of the largest festivals Yakamas shared with other people was held in May and June, around what is today the town of Kittitas (near Ellensburg, Washington). The site was an important camas root-digging area and the get-together came at the end of several weeks of digging enough roots to feed tribal members through the coming winter.

One white fur trader saw this celebration in the 1800s and described it in his journal as being so big that the festival area covered at least six miles. The trader said there must have been over 3,000 men, plus women and children, attending.

Many groups gathered at the south end of Lake Cle Elum to fish for salmon and to party. Another big inter-tribal get-together took place in early August, when people gathered camas-plant roots, one of the most important foods of the Yakama people. The yearly gatherings, like those hosted by the Yakama tribal nation, show that although small fights might break out at times between neighboring villages and tribes, they were mainly peaceful, generous people.

Not only were rituals of thanksgiving for food celebrated at feasts but games of chance were played; traders showed their wares; and athletic contests always were held between villagers and their guests. Wrestling matches, foot races, and, later on, horse races were held. Especially enjoyed was a popular game called *shinney,* which is much like our modern game of field hockey.

Objects used in playing all games came from nature. Such things as nuts, rocks, pine cones, seeds, leaves, feathers, beaver teeth, and berries became dice, balls, and hockey pucks. Children played their own games, which were much like those the adults played.

## TRADING

One of the most exciting parts of a celebration was the trading that went on between a host village and its visitors. Those invited to feasts always brought with them trading items which they thought a host village might need or want. Host villages, in turn, always had a ready supply of goods they could trade.

Traders went about their business whether there was a feast or not. Plateau traders would journey long distances to neighboring tribes, going as far west as possible to trade. They exchanged not only goods but ideas with other villages, as well.

Some traders traveled by land, walking and using *travois* to carry their supplies of trading goods. A *travois's* poles were cut to different length, so they did not bounce together each time they passed over uneven, rocky ground. This was a clever way to make a *travois* travel more smoothly. A smoother trip meant fewer fragile trading goods being broken as traders journeyed from village to village. Before horses, *travois* were pulled by trained dogs. Later, horses themselves became a favored trading goods.

Tribal members in the southwest part of our country were the first to trade with Spanish explorers for horses and to begin raising their own herds. Plateau tribal members traded with the Plains bands to get their first horses. By the 1800s horse-trading had become very popular in the Northwest.

*Dogs were used by Native Americans to carry their belongings until horses arrived on this continent with the Spanish explorers. Plateau people first traded for horses with Plains tribes in the 1700s.*

What the Plains bands wanted most, in trade for the horses, were the Plateau hunters' beautifully made bows. Plains hunters felt Plateau bows were much better designed and made than their own.

Yakama traders also traveled by pine or cottonwood dugout canoes to riverside places where there were many other traders. One of the largest trading areas in North America was on the Columbia River at The Dalles, Oregon. From there they boated downriver to as far west as the Pacific Coast trading centers. Yakima people were especially interested in getting dried fish and seal meat, whale blubber, fish and whale oils, and other products coastal tribes had to offer.

Coastal tribes traded for such Plateau goods as buffalo skins, furs, elkskin robes, mountain goat wool, baskets, basket hats, and weaving materials such as bear grass, spruce roots, and feathers. Foods found in the drier, hotter country east of the Cascade Mountains, including dried roots, berries, and pemmican were a welcome change for coastal peoples' meals.

If a trader had no goods to offer for something he wanted, he then used the tribal form of money, measured strings of dentalium shells. These small, delicate seashells were found only off the west coast of Vancouver Island. The more perfectly matched shells that were in a string, the more value it had. Especially fine dentalium shells were so valuable that they were used for clothing decorations and jewelry, such as necklaces and earrings.

Traders came from as far away as Alaska, the Midwestern plains, and northern California just to trade for Northwest tribal goods. Dentalium shells have been found as far south as along the southern coast of California, where they were so valuable, only wealthy California tribespeople could afford to own them.

## RELIGION

Yakama people practiced religion everyday, in every part of life. They believed that all objects around them, from the wind to small rocks, had spirit power. Villagers felt even birds and animals had their own songs and language. For that reason, tribal people were careful never to make spirits angry by taking too much from the land or using more of nature's gifts than they needed.

When children became old enough to take care of themselves, perhaps between the ages of seven through ten, they were sent alone on a 'vision quest' into the mountains. They would stay in their chosen holy place for as long as they could stand it, hoping for a guardian spirit to appear. Sometimes they stayed only one night; some youngsters remained in their holy place for several days. Those who found a spirit guardian were considered to have special power.

Children never spoke of their spiritual guardian when they returned home. If a child showed he or she had received a guardian, only shamans (spiritual doctors) were allowed to explain its power to a child.

Such a spiritual power was important to young Yakama children. It told them how to dress, how to paint their faces for celebrations, and most important, how to behave in everyday life. Children receiving a guardian on their 'vision quest' were given the honor of joining adults in ritual dancing and singing during special winter religious ceremonies. They danced and sang to the rhythm of long plank drums hit with tall canes or sticks during the pure religious faith ceremonies known as 'longhouse rituals.' Many times these children later became shamans or spiritual doctors.

Yakama people believed that if they did bad things, a spirit could make them sick or cause them to have terrible accidents. When this happened a medical spirit doctor, thought to have special powers, was called to cure the illness or injury. Shamans used objects from nature, such as bear claws, wolf headdresses, or deer dew-claw rattles, to help them with their curing. Dew-claws are the smaller claws found on the legs above and behind the foot hooves; much like those found on dogs' legs.

Shamans used many ways to cure a sick person. A visit to the sweathouse to steam sickness away, probably was the first method tried by villagers to cure themselves. Some carried with them a piece of wild rosebush believing it would keep away ghosts and evil spirits they felt had caused their illness. Tribal members also tried to keep away from owls, which they believed were bad omens telling them of sickness or death coming soon.

Sometimes an herbal tea was brewed for the ill person to drink. Women shamans were especially good with plant and herbal teas that cured. Many of the plants and herbs used by ancient Yakama doctors are still used today by modern doctors.

Healing doctors often placed hands upon the part of a body which was hurt, massaging the body and saying prayers. Other times they sucked on a body's hurt area through a tube, hoping to draw any pain out the tube and back to the spirit who had caused it. Some spirit doctors used only dancing and singing to remove pain.

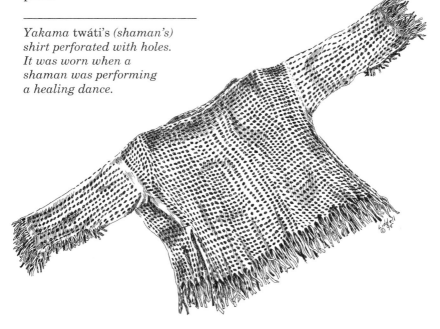

*Yakama* twáti's *(shaman's)*
*shirt perforated with holes.*
*It was worn when a*
*shaman was performing*
*a healing dance.*

Shamans often specialized in certain areas of power. For instance, some were best known for predicting weather, while others might be good at finding lost items or predicting the future.

Religious areas, called shrines, were usually found in lonely places so people could say prayers privately. Special shrines were found in the center of Yakama territory, where all tribal members could travel to leave token offerings, or gifts, to their spirits.

Yakama ritual ceremonies were serious ways of honoring all powers. Those attending ritual events wore their most beautiful clothes. Women's soft buckskin dresses were long, to the heels, and decorated with feathers and shell beads. Their moccasins and leggings were trimmed in color, and they wore the finest dentalium necklaces they owned. Many times women painted their faces red.

Men wore buckskin shirts, pants decorated with porcupine quills and designs picturing their dreams and visions of guardian spirits. Their moccasins and leggings were trimmed in red. Men painted their faces red and yellow, wore short bonnet headdresses made of beautiful feathers, and hung strings of dentalia shells or wampum shells around their necks. Hair was usually tied upward into a piece of animal fur.

## CLOTHING

Everyday clothes were not nearly as bright and colorful as religious ceremonial clothing. Before there were horses to help hunters kill more animals, Plateau women made clothing by shredding the bark of cedar, willow trees, or sagebrush, then weaving the bark into fabric for clothing.

With the arrival of horses, mounted hunters were able to kill enough deer, elk, as well as smaller hides of wolves, coyotes, bears, and foxes for warmer winter clothing. The thick-haired skins of otter, beaver, and mink had always given tribal members especially warm clothing. Now hunters could provide enough thick layers of buffalo and elk skins to make clothing and blankets for all tribal members during the plateau region's icy-cold winters.

Horses arrived with European explorers, and Native American hunters knew right away that these animals would change their lives for the better. Now hunters could travel faster, shooting their bows and arrows from horseback. Now they could kill bigger animals, such as buffalo, in larger numbers and shoot from greater distances, making it easier and safer for hunters to do their jobs.

Women, thanks to the horse, could now wear dresses from the skins of two deer, instead of one. These newer-style dresses usually reached to the ankles and were sewn down each side. Shoulder seams could be either laced together or stitched.

The soft-skin, hairless short shirts women made for their families were styled to come down to the waist. Each shirt was cut from one oblong piece of hide which had a neck hole cut in the center of it. Sometimes short sleeves were set in before sewing up the sides. Usually a seam was decorated with fringe. Often shell beads were strung onto the fringes.

The skin breechclout (a leather apron) continued to be worn by men in hot weather as in olden days. During the winters, men wore soft-hide pants with fringes on the outside pants seam. Children dressed like adults; however, they wore very little clothing, if any, in the summer's heat.

Necklaces were worn by both men and women. Less colorful shell beads, elks' teeth, and porcupine quills were worn for everyday decorations and more valuable jewelry, like dentalia shells, were worn for ceremonies.

Both men and women wore their hair long. Sometimes it was braided. Other times they tied it into a ponytail at the back of the neck with a length of rawhide or a thin piece of rope. Not all tribespeople wore their hair the same way; each village or tribelet had its own hairstyle.

## FOOD

Yakama territory weather had four distinct seasons, causing the villagers to travel, throughout the year, from place to place to gather food as it ripened. By moving around, fresh foods were found in every season but winter.

During the summer, villagers would gather wild vegetable greens, grasses, and berries. When autumn arrived, the women used some preserved fish and meat along with fresh meats. Most winter meals were made up of preserved fish, meats, roots, and berries. Springtime once again brought delicious fresh green vegetables and grasses and the first salmon run of the year. Salmon, the best source of food for Yakama villagers, was eaten in some form all year long.

The camas lily bulb was a very important plant food to Yakama people, second only to salmon as their main food. These starchy bulbs were eaten raw, roasted, or ground into a flour (see page 41) to make cakes, which were then boiled before being eaten. As explained under Village Life, huge celebrations, called first-food festivals, were given by the Yakamas each spring at the camas root-gathering camps.

Special digging sticks, called kupins, whose tips had been hardened by placing them in fires, were used to remove bulbs from the ground. The sticks had antler handles on one end while the digging end had a slight curve so it would not cut through a root or bulb. With a little pressure on the stick from a woman's hands, it could pop a root above-ground. The root was then placed in a net bag tied around the gatherer's waist. Digging sticks also helped the women harvest wild carrots, wild onions, bitterroot, and other underground foods.

The last first-food ceremony of the year was held in August at food camps near the Cascade foothills. It was held to honor huckleberries, a favorite berry of the tribe. Huckleberries were gathered and carried back to camp. There they were placed on a smoldering log to dry. Dried berries were put in folded and sewn cedar bark to store for winter meals. Often times they were mixed with dried buffalo meat and animal fat to become what tribal people called pemmican, a wholesome, tasty winter treat.

For over 4,500 years, Yakama villagers built most of their year around salmon. Salmon runs came twice a year (spring and autumn.) No fisherman was allowed to catch salmon for his family until after the first-salmon ceremony. Yakama people believed that if someone ate salmon meat before thanks had been given to the creator, the salmon would not return to the rivers.

Salmon provided 90% of all the tribe's food. Although salmon was the favorite fish, native fishermen also caught trout and giant sturgeon.

## PREPARING FOOD

Yakama women cooked food in many ways. In-the-ground baking pits were dug when the food had to be cooked for long periods of time. A pit was dug and lined with leaves women gathered from the ground. Rocks, heated in the fire overnight, were put on the bottom of the pit. Food to be cooked was wrapped in fresh leaves and placed atop the rocks. Then soil was packed on top

*Baking pits used by Yakama women for slow-baking food.*

of the rocks and food, where it cooked much like we cook in a modern-day slow cooker. Breads and bulbs were often cooked this way.

Pit-baking was begun in the morning and was a good way for small groups of people, moving from place to place during gathering trips, to have a meal ready when they came back to their camp in the evening. Everything from fish to bread-like cakes could be cooked this way.

Fresh foods that needed to be roasted or broiled were attached to the end of a thick stick and propped over an open fire. Boiling was done by stirring heated rocks through uncooked food which had been placed in a basket. Small sticks were used to toss the rocks until the food was cooked. Constantly tossing hot rocks kept the cooking basket from burning.

## BASKETS

Yakama women were well-known for their excellent baskets. They used either a twining method to make a more open weave basket or the more complicated coiling method. A coiling weave took longer to do, but coiled baskets could be more tightly woven. Coiled baskets were also stiffer and held their shape better than most twined baskets.

All native women would have had a much harder time doing their work if they hadn't had baskets. Not only were baskets used for gathering plant foods but were needed for cooking and storing foods as well. Many baskets were so tightly woven that foods could be boiled in water in them without their leaking.

*A soft-woven bag made by tribes located near The Dalles, along the banks of the Columbia River. Called Sally bags after a woman of the Wasco band, who was thought to have been the first basket weaver to decorate her baskets in this manner. Corn husk fibers were used to create colored decorations. The top edge of this basket is bound with deerskin.*

Family belongings were kept in large baskets, making moving from one food camp to another much simpler. Smaller, beautifully-decorated coiled baskets were used to store personal treasures or for trade with other tribes.

The women twined soft, cylinder-shaped baskets, called Sally bags, to carry roots as they were collected. The baskets were decorated with human or animal-figure designs and were made from bear grass.

Large, flat, twined baskets, known as cornhusk bags, were made for hauling and storing roots. They were twined from fibers of the Indian hemp plant and got their name, 'cornhusk bags,' from the dyed cornhusk decorations that were sewn onto the front of them. Cornhusk bags could be folded flat and put away when they were not in use.

Yakama women were also famous for their hard, tightly coiled baskets which were used to hold huge amounts of fruit, berries, or roots. Called Klikitat baskets, this style was named for a smaller band of people living near the Yakamas but was actually made by most Plateau region women. Klikitat baskets usually were woven from cedar roots and were decorated with designs made from dyed ryegrass.

# FISHING AND HUNTING

## FISHING

The art of basket-making was also used in weaving fish traps. When explorers Captain Meriwether Lewis and Captain William Clark arrived in the early 1800s, they found Plateau fishermen using the basketry traps, along with many other excellent methods, to catch fish.

Lewis and Clark also wrote of native fishermen building weirs across smaller streams to catch fish. A weir was a willow-brush or stone fence with only one opening in it. A basketry fish trap was placed at the opening to catch fish as they tried to swim through. Sometimes a fisherman stood at the opening spearing fish. Other times nets or pens were built at the opening of a weir.

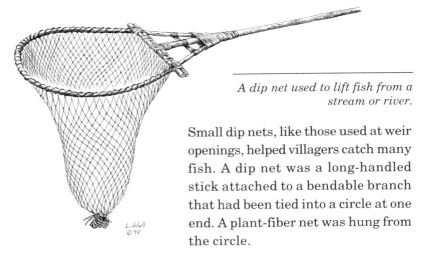

*A dip net used to lift fish from a stream or river.*

Small dip nets, like those used at weir openings, helped villagers catch many fish. A dip net was a long-handled stick attached to a bendable branch that had been tied into a circle at one end. A plant-fiber net was hung from the circle.

Larger fish, such as salmon and sturgeon, were caught with two-prong harpoons or with spears made with detachable stone points. Lewis and Clark also described the fishers as using stone weights to hold nets down in the water, which they dragged behind their wooden dugout canoes to collect fish. Modern fishers still use this kind of method for hauling in fish today.

The dugout canoes used for transportation and fishing by Yakama people were usually made by first burning, then digging out the insides of logs. This kind of canoe measured about two feet across and was from 12 to 30 feet long.

Native Americans living near the Columbia River had a sacred fishing area called Celilo Falls. People had been living at the falls for some 8,000 years. Here the river was shallow and ran over rocks, causing the water to cascade in small falls. Native fishermen built wooden platforms far out over the water and speared salmon as the fish made

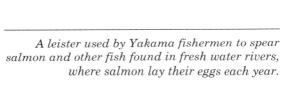

*A leister used by Yakama fishermen to spear salmon and other fish found in fresh water rivers, where salmon lay their eggs each year.*

their way upstream to spawn. Lewis and Clark wrote in their journals about tribal people catching and drying as many as 30,000 pounds of salmon a year at the falls.

However, in this century huge dams have been built across the Columbia River to produce electric power for our needs. When The Dalles Dam was completed some 40 years ago, Celilo Falls was covered with many feet of water.

Although the United States government had promised to let tribal members keep their sacred fishing grounds forever, this promise has been broken. Native American people mourn the loss of their fishing site.

What's more, many environmental experts now believe a recent serious drop in the number of salmon found in the Northwest has been because of the many dams built on the Columbia River. Salmon cannot swim upstream to spawn as easily as they used to do.

## HUNTING

Plateau hunters used bows and arrows for at least three thousand years before rifles, bought from European traders, became the Native Americans' favorite hunting weapon. Most hunters made their excellent bows from oak wood. Bow strings were usually made of elk *sinew,* which was treated in special ways to keep it from stretching too much or breaking when the bow was strung.

The best Plateau arrows were made from branches of the serviceberry bush. So many arrows were made from this kind of bush that the Native Americans actually called it by the name of 'arrow bush' in their language. The wood was lightweight, straight, and hard, the best kind of wood to make arrows go straight to their targets.

Arrowheads were small and chipped from obsidian, a volcanic glass that came in trade from the Northern Paiute band of people living near what is Bend, Oregon today. Yakama hunters reworked the bits of obsidian by placing them on soft elk hide and, using pressure with an elk-antler flaking tool, shaped the

*Feathers at the end of an arrow were needed to allow the flying arrow to go in a straight line for the target. This is called fletching.*

arrowheads until they were the proper shape and size. These obsidian tips were then attached to the arrow with an Indian-hemp string sealed with sticky pine-tree pitch.

Most important on each arrow was the placement of feathers at the end. This art was called *fletching*. The direction an arrow went depended on where these cut-off feathers were placed. Because the job was so hard, it took many years for a grandson to learn from his grandfather important skills in the art of making and using weapons. A young Native American boy knew that when he was grown, his family would depend upon his ability to hunt if they were to be well-fed and warmly-clothed for winter.

## OTHER TOOLS AND UTENSILS

As with all Native Americans, the Yakama people made tools from objects found in nature around them. Rocks were always found near them and were a part of everyday life. Heated stones were used to form steam in sweathouses and for cooking food. Heavy rocks weighted down fishnets.

Special flat-shaped rocks were used as mortars and long, cylinder-shaped rocks became pestles when they served as grinding tools. Women used stone mortars and pestles to grind seeds into flour and herbs into powder for herbal tea. Sharp-edged rocks became knife blades, arrow heads, or animal-skin scrapers.

Animal bones never went to waste. Tiny bird bones could be made into whistles or splintered into needles. Leg bones of small animals could also be made into musical whistles. Larger-animal knuckles, like those of elk, made excellent spoons to use for eating. Bone splinters with sharp points were made into needles for sewing clothing together, and antlers were used as wedges for splitting logs into planks. Antlers also were strong enough to use in flaking obsidian into arrowheads.

Wood was used to build framework for homes and platforms over water for fishing. Small pieces of wood could be carved into combs. Small wooden mortars and pestles were used in grinding softer things like herbal plants. But especially, wood was needed to keep fires burning for heat and cooking.

# HISTORY

As white people began to settle in the far-western part of the United States, tribespeople there began having real problems with settlers taking their ancient food-gathering and sacred lands, claiming it as their own. The United States government often was at fault, giving tribal lands to settlers without first getting permission from tribal owners.

At first the Yakama people did not have to worry about white settlers because their land was too dry to farm. Early settlers were more interested in land near what is today called the Willamette Valley in Oregon. However, in the mid-1800s, the United States government claimed land which had been known as 'Oregon Territory', (now the states of Washington and Oregon) as a part of the United States. This land included Yakama territory.

White settlers began arriving in Eastern Washington and original tribal owners, who had owned the land for thousands of years, began having serious trouble with the government over who really owned the land. A treaty was was finally drawn up between Oregon Territory Plateau tribes and the U.S. Congress in 1855.

It took Congress four more years to approve the treaty. In the meantime, Washington territory governor, Isaac I. Stevens, illegally allowed white families to settle on tribal land. As a result, fierce wars were fought and many Native American leaders, as well as government soldiers, lost their lives because of the confusion. Kamiakin, one of the few remaining Yakama chiefs alive after the many wars, was forced to flee to Canada to escape death. He lived the rest of his life in Canada, away from his homeland.

As a part of the treaty, when it was finally ratified, the federal government set aside a reservation for the Yakamas. By 1860, many Yakama people had begun to settle on the reservation. They had lost the most respected of their leaders, including Kamiakin, during those terrible years but they were together again.

# CONCLUSION

Today's Yakama people are well-organized and now go by the name of Confederated Tribes and Bands of the Yakama Indian Nation. Their reservation has its own laws, court, and a police force to keep order, in their own manner, on the reservation. Tribal members continue to follow many of the traditional beliefs and still celebrate some of the old religious ceremonies. They still eat many of the traditional foods; they fish, hunt, and gather huckleberries and special roots throughout the seasons of the year, as their ancestors did before them.

The Yakama nation's present-day leadership is headed by a tribal council, which elects new members every four years. Council members are active in tribal business and in 1972 were able to recover ownership of Mt. Adams from the United States government. Yakama people consider this mountain a part of their tribe's past, present, and future. They feel Mt. Adams is a symbol of their tribe's strength.

Council members handle all the natural resources of their reservation but they must present their wishes to the federal government over and over again, in order to be sure of having even as important a resource as water from nearby rivers to serve those living on the reservation.

The Yakamas believe in giving their children an excellent education. Many tribal youngsters attend nearby public schools; however, the tribal council has worked with the state of Washington to provide a few public grade schools on the reservation itself. Students at the reservation schools have Yakama history woven into American history classes. There are elective classes in Yakama arts, singing, and drumming. Student fieldtrips include root digging and huckleberry picking.

Teaching of the Yakama language is an important part of reservation schools. The Yakama language is also taught at tribal summer schools to those who do not study it in their regular schools. Older tribal members still tell ancient tribal legends to those children attending summer school. Summer evenings find young people sitting around campfires, listening to ancient legends from their elders.

Young tribal adults now have their own college to attend when they graduate from high school. By 1995, Heritage College had awarded 600 college degrees, currently has 1,200 students, and one of its own graduates serves as the college's attorney.

Today's Yakama nation has a magnificent Cultural Heritage Center, a compound of several buildings, which opened in 1980 in the town of Toppenish, Washington. Included in the center is a fine library, a gift shop for visitors, and a restaurant featuring many native foods. Tourists may visit a large, well-done museum where replicas of the mat-covered lodges of the old days are shown, as are many of the ancient tools and utensils that were important to long-ago tribal life.

In the center of the compound's buildings, the 75-foot-tall roof of the tribal nation's large winter lodge stands out against the sky. This community hall is used for special tribal meetings, feasts, and conventions. Part of the reservation is private and only seen by tribal members. The council sees that no trespassers are found on this private land.

Unlike many other Native American groups in our country today, Yakama tribespeople still live on the reservation assigned to them nearly 150 years ago by the United States government. Even more important to them, the reservation is located on a piece of their ancient territory. Although their land today is only a small part of the original territory, at least tribal members are able to say there have been Yakama people living on some part of their land for at least the past 12,000 years.

# YAKAMA OUTLINE

I. Introduction
    A. Location and climate of Plateau region
    B. Plants growing there and uses
        1. Importance of sagebrush
    C. Rivers of region and their importance
    D. Creator legend of Yakama people

II. Villages
    A. Location of villages and why
    B. Population of villages
    C. Number of buildings in village
    D. Description of buildings in permanent villages
        1. Pit houses
        2. New **A**-shaped mat lodges
        3. Sweatlodges, location and description

III. Village life
    A. Men and women's jobs
    B. Chief and leaders of village
        1. How chosen and duties of leaders
    C. Marriage
    D. Childbirth and childhood
        1. Training of children by parents and grandparents
    E. Teen-age ceremonies

IV. Feasts and Celebrations
    A. Root-digging celebrations
    B. Fishing feasts
    C. Games

V. Trading
    A. At feasts and on the road
    B. Transportation
        1. Travois and dogs vs horses
    C. Items traded and "money" used

VI. Religion
    A. Beliefs about nature
    B. Children's "vision quests"
    C. Kinds of shamans
    D. Shrines
    E. Ritual ceremonies and costumes

VII. Clothing
    A. Kinds of fabric used in clothes
    B. Types of animal hides used
    C. Women's, Men's, and children's clothing styles
    D. Jewelry and hairstyles for adults

VIII. Food
    A. Fresh food in all four seasons
    B. Cooking and preparing food
        1. Pit-baking, roasting, broiling, and boiling
IX. Baskets, descriptions and uses
    A. Importance of cornhusk bags
    B. Treasure baskets
X. Hunting and Fishing
    A. Fishing
        1. Traps and weirs, dip, gill and seine nets
        2. Dugout canoe description
        3. Celilo Falls and its loss to Yakamas
    B. Hunting
        1. Descriptions of bows and arrows
            a. Arrowheads
            b. Fletching
        2. Other tools and utensils
            a. Kinds made of stone
            b. Use of bone for tools and utensils
            c. Use of wood
XI. History
    A. Losing territory to white settlers
        1. Missionaries come to Eastern Washington
        2. Native American treaty with the U.S. Congress in 1860
            a. Governor Stevens, War treaties, and Chief
               Kamiakin
        3. Reservation
XII. Conclusion
    A. Modern government of Yakama Nation and its name
        1. Tribal Council
    B. Mt. Adams ownership returned to tribe
    C. Education of today's Yakama children
        1. Children's reservation schools and summer schools
        2. Reteaching of Yakama language
        3. Heritage College
    D. Cultural Center description

# GLOSSARY

Adze:  An axe-like tool used for carving or shaping wood

Anthropologist:  A scientist who studies the ways of life of humans now and long ago

Awl:  A sharp, pointed tool used for making small holes in leather or wood

Coiling:  A way of weaving baskets which looks like the basket is made of rope coils woven together

Culture:  The behaviors, living patterns, and products of a group of people

Dialect:  Ways of speaking a language in different parts of a country, like a Southern accent or a western cowboy twang

Dip net:  A fishing net with long handles.  Woven netting was attached to a thin willow branch, bent and tied into a circle.  A handle was then attached to the branch.

Drought:  A long period of time without rain

Dwelling:  A building where people live

Fasting:  Going without food and/or water

Fletching:  Feathers attached to the back end of an arrow

Fresh-water:  Water from rivers or streams; water which contains no salt

Gill net:  A flat net hanging vertically in water to catch fish by their heads or gills

Heir:  A person or persons who are given the belongings of someone who has died

Heritage:  Something passed down to people, whether it be a talent or object, from their long-ago relatives

Hibernating:  To spend each winter sleeping, as a bear does

Mortar:  Flat surface of wood or stone; used with a pestle (see below) for the grinding of foods, medicines, etc.

Nomadic:  Without a home; moving from place to place

Pestle:  A stone club used in a mortar to mash, pound, or grind

Quiver:  Holder for arrows

Reservation:  Land set aside for Native Americans by the United States government

# **GLOSSARY** (continued)

Rite or Ritual:   A ceremony that is always performed the same way

Run of fish:   When fish return to fresh water where they were spawned (born)

Shaft:   The stick part of an arrow

Shaman:   Man or woman believed to be in direct contact with spirits

Siene net:   A long fishing net which hangs vertically in the water, encircling and trapping fish when it is pulled together

Sinew:   Stretchy tendons of animals

Spawn:   The eggs laid by fish

Territory:   Land owned by someone or something

Theory:   A researched guess about something

Travois:   A frame slung between two poles to carry belongings; pulled by an animal, usually a dog or horse

Trespassing:   Entering a territory without permission

Twining:   A method of weaving baskets by twisting fibers, rather than coiling them  around a support fiber

Wampum:   Polished shell beads strung on string and used as money by Native Americans

# NATIVE AMERICAN WORDS WE KNOW AND USE

## PLANTS AND TREES

hickory
pecan
yucca
mesquite
saguaro

## ANIMALS

caribou
chipmunk
cougar
jaguar
opossum
moose

## STATES

Dakota – friend
Ohio – good river
Minnesota – waters that
   reflect the sky
Oregon – beautiful water
Nebraska – flat water
Arizona
Texas

## FOODS

avocado
hominy
maize (corn)
persimmon
tapioca
succotash

## GEOGRAPHY

bayou – marshy body of water
savannah – grassy plain
pasadena – valley

## WEATHER

blizzard
Chinook (warm, dry wind)

## FURNITURE

hammock

## HOUSE

wigwam
wickiup
tepee
igloo

## INVENTIONS

toboggan

## BOATS

canoe
kayak

## OTHER WORDS

caucus – group meeting
mugwump – loner politician
squaw – woman
papoose – baby

## CLOTHING

moccasin
parka
mukluk – slipper
poncho

# YAKAMA BIBLIOGRAPHY

Carpenter, Cecilla Svinth. *They Walked Before.* Washinton State American Revolution Bicentennial Commission. Tacoma, WA: 1977.

Cressman, L.S.. *Prehistory of the Far West.* Salt Lake City, Utah: University of Utah Press, 1977.

Hunn, Eugene S. *Nch'i - Wána The Big River.* Seattle, WA and London: University of WA Press, 1990.

Jacobson, Daniel. *Great Indian Tribes.* Maplewood, NJ: Hammond, Inc., 1970.

Lobb, Allen. *Indian Baskets of the Pacific Northwest and Alaska.* Portland, OR : Graphic Arts Center Publishing Co., 1992.

Ruby, R.H. and Brown, John A.. *Indians of the Pacific Northwest.* Norman, Oklahoma: University of Oklahoma Press, 1981.

Schuster, Helen H.. *The Yakima.* New York & Philadelphia: Chelsea House Publishers, 1990.

Sherrow, Victoria. *Indians of the Plateau and Great Basin.* First American Series. New York, NY: Benford Books, Inc., 1992.

Washington State Superintendent of Public Education, Judith Billings. *Indians of Washington State.* Olympia, WA: 1993.

# GENERAL BIOGRAPHY

Billard, Jules B. ed. *The World of the American Indian.* Washington, D.C.:National Geographic Society, 1989

Boulé, Mary Null. *California Native American Tribes.* 26 vols. Vashon, WA: Merryant Publishers, Inc., 1993.

Brandon, William. *Indians.* Renewed copyright, Boston, MA: Houghton Mifflin Co., 1989 .

Franklin, Paula A.. *Indians of North America.* New York, NY: David McKay Company, Inc., 1979.

Goodchild, Peter. *Survival Skills of the North American Indians.* Chicago, IL: Chicago Review Press, 1984.

Jones, Jayne C.. *The American Indian in America.* Minneapolis, MN: Lerner Publications Co., 1973.

Josephy, Alvin M., Jr.. *The Indian Heritage of America.* Boston, MA: Houghton Mifflin, 1991.

Maxwell, James A.. *America's Fascinating Indian Heritage.* Pleasantville,NY and Montreal, Canada: The Reader's Digest Assoc., Inc., 1978.

Nabokov, Peter, and Easton, Robert. *Native American Architecture.* New York, NY and Oxford, England: Oxford University Press, 1989.

Owens, Royce C., Deetz, J.J.F., and Fisher, O.D.. *The North American Indians.* New York, NY: The Macmillan Co., 1967.

# **GENERAL BIOGRAPHY** (continued)

Reimer, Henry. *Indian Country.* Minneapolis, MN: T.S. Denison and Co., Inc., 1973.

Sturtevant, Wm. C., General ed. *Handbook Of North American Indians,* Vols.V, VI, VII,VIII, IX, X, XI, XV. Washington D.C.: Smithsonian Institute, US Government Printing Office, 1978 - 1990.

Sturtevant, Wm. C. and Taylor, Colin F. consultants. *The Native Americans.* New York, NY: Smithmark Publications (Salamander Books), 1992.

Taylor, Colin F.. *Native American Life.* New York, NY 10016: Smithmark Publishers, 1996.

Time-Life Editors, Thomas H. Flaherty, editor-in-chief. *The American Indians.* Alexandria, VA: Time-Life Books, 1992.

Tunis, Edward. *Indians.* Cleveland, OH and New York, NY: The World Publishing Co. , 1959.

Turnbaugh, S.P, and Wm. A.. *Indian Baskets.* Westchester, PA: Schiffer Publishers, Ltd., 1986.

Waldman, Carl. *Atlas of the North American Indian.* New York, NY: Factson File, 1985.

Yellow Robe, Rosebud. *An Album of the American Indians.* New York, NY: Franklin Watts, Inc., 1969.

**Credits:**

Dona McAdam, Mac on the Hill, Seattle, Washington 98109

**Special thanks**

Mary Basta for her artwork on pages 29, 39, 42, and 49.